12/25/93
To my two
Favorite Delaware
natives - Merry X-Mas.
Love,
Ted

DELAWARE

DISCOVERED

Undaunted by the elements, Caesar Rodney dashed 90 miles from Dover to Philadelphia one stormy
July night in 1776 to swing Delaware's vote at the Second Continental Congress in favor of U.S. Independence.
He gallops today in Wilmington's Rodney Square.
End Sheet: Towering 441 feet over the Delaware River, the twin spans of Delaware Memorial Bridge
gateway the second smallest state — 96 miles long and at most 35 miles wide.

Kevin Fleming

Legends by Karl Harr · Edited by Jane Vessels

ISBN 0-929518-15-2
Library of Congress Catalog Card Number 92-081527

Photographed in 1982 for National Geographic, Dover's mighty C5 Galaxie fleet — aircraft large enough to carry six tour busses — distinguished itself during Operation Desert Storm.

His last wishes honored, the bulk of Nutter D. Marvel's horse-drawn carriage collection remain in the Georgetown museum he founded. Marvel died in 1988.

pparently you *can* go home again. Thanks to an assignment from Delaware Governor Mike Castle I had the opportunity to get reacquainted with my home state — ten years after I had photographed a *National Geographic* story that grew into a book, *Delaware, Small Wonder.*

In the decade since *Small Wonder*, magazine and book assignments have taken me to the North Pole, New Zealand, China, the Mediterranean, Europe, and East Africa. I've traveled by dogsled across Canada's Northwest Territories, on foot with Somali nomads, and by airboat in the Florida Everglades. Yet after all this I've found that my favorite place to work as a photographer is where I started, at home in Delaware.

What do people think when they hear the word Delaware? In my travels — even in the United States — I've had to remind people where it is, and even that it exists. No wonder Delaware is a popular category on the quiz show Jeopardy!

I'm sure that for many people traveling between New York City and Washington, D.C., the state is only a twelve-mile stretch of I-95 with a toll booth at either end. But if they would stray from their high-speed course I think they would be surprised by the variety of the second smallest state.

*Clapboard siding and fishscale shingles
on a farmhouse near Bowers Beach
have been replaced with modern siding.*

Wilmington, the largest city and seat of New Castle County, has grown with the state's new identity as a center of the financial services industries. I found that my former employer, the *News-Journal*, had moved south into the county while new businesses like Chemical Bank have moved in, adding sleek profiles to the city's skyline.

Even with a greater population and increasingly cosmopolitan atmosphere, Wilmington retains the openness of a small town. Whether you're ordering a turkey sub at Capriotti's or a filet in the Green Room of the Hotel Du Pont, the friendliness hasn't changed.

One of my favorite drives in the state is Route 9, a two lane "Scenic Route" following the Delaware River and Bay. The sign at its northern terminus near Delaware City announcing "Scenic Route Ends" always makes me laugh – Delaware's only refinery looms in the background. The state decided in 1971 that one refinery was enough and passed the landmark Coastal Zone Act, prohibiting new heavy industry along the environmentally sensitive river and bay. I am afraid to think what the coast might look like today if that legislation had not passed.

4

One of my favorite subjects for many years,
the Port Mahon Lighthouse, built in
the early 19th century, could not survive
a vandal's match.

Frank Perdue's poultry empire, already
very big business in 1982, has crossed
the Mississippi River and expanded to the
Pacific Coast.

A classic understatement, an official
state highway sign continues to mark the
spot along Route 9 near Delaware City
where the rural South meets an urban,
industrial North.

Travelling downstate you pass thousands of acres of wetlands on the east, miles of corn and soybeans on farmland to the west. The past decade doesn't seem to have changed small towns like Port Penn — probably liveliest when it's serving up plates of muskrat for its fall Marsh Festival.

Farther south, the road enters Kent County and passes Leipsic, home of the crab eaters' mecca — Sambo's Tavern. Amazingly, I have twice met people in Europe who had eaten there.

I found Leipsic waterman Harry Killen cracking walnuts in his backyard, waiting for the spring crab season to begin. I would have found him in the same place ten years ago. Now in his 70s, Harry will still head out to the bay to start crabbing before dawn.

Delaware's fields of soybeans and corn become chicken feed for its broiler industry, centered in Sussex County. Health-conscious consumers ate more chicken in the 1980s and those higher poultry sales have now made agriculture Delaware's top industry.

Retracing a lifetime of steps around the state has made me realize that there is not one spot I can single out as my favorite. Diversity is one of Delaware's great gifts. An hour south from the grand estates and rolling, stone-walled countryside of the Brandywine River Valley you find the carriages of Amish farmers and the protected marshlands of Bombay Hook National Wildlife Refuge. Another hour south and you're on an Atlantic beach, surf casting for bluefish or strolling the Rehoboth Beach boardwalk.

Despite the growth — new roads I'd never driven, new housing developments where I knew farmland — Delaware still feels more like a small town to me than a state. It is not unusual for a citizen to personally know the entire contingent to the U.S. House of Representatives — there's only one. And the governor is more likely to be addressed by first name than formal title.

I miss that. I hope the images on the following pages will tell you many stories about this special place in America that is very special to me. — Kevin Fleming

NEW CASTLE

Overlooking Delaware's rolling
northern countryside, a water tower
rises 112 steps above an estate in
Chateau Country. Though smallest of
Delaware's three counties, New Castle
is home to two-thirds of the state's
680,000 people. Balancing the two
faces of Delaware, it is the center of
industry and commerce, yet is as rural
as muskrat marshes and pastures of
grazing thoroughbreds.

8

The flow of events leading to Delaware's leadership in industrial research began on the Brandywine River north of Wilmington. The rapids powered Walker's Mill, a textile producer from 1815 to the late 1930s,

as well as flour mills, mills for paper, snuff, and linseed oil, and — starting in 1803 — a gunpowder mill for an French immigrant family named du Pont.

One of the nation's busiest corridors, I-95 and its spur routes linked Wilmington with the burgeoning
East Coast in the mid-1960s. Delaware's largest city, population 72,000, saw its skyline soar in the early

1980s as new state laws attracted financial institutions to this longtime center of the chemical industry and corporate law.

A dawn workout heralds a day at the races at Delaware Park in Stanton. Admired as one of the most beautiful in the U.S., the thoroughbred track hosts the $150,000 Delaware Handicap each July, and also

races Arabians. Following pages: Horses hot from the fox hunt were once bathed in the shower room of a Centerville barn with water pumped from its tower.

With a big city face and a small town soul, Wilmington grew along an orderly grid design borrowed from Philadelphia, visible on the horizon nearly 30 miles up the Delaware River.

The Dutch were the first Europeans in the region, but Swedes built the first permanent settlement, introducing log cabins to the New World here in 1638.

Swedish governor Johan Rising wrote home in 1654: "If a law-reader could be sent here, it would be desirable." His wish has been amply answered. Much of modern corporate law has been forged in the state's Chancery Court. More than half of the top 500 U.S. companies and a third of the companies on the New York Stock Exchange are incorporated here because of low fees and top legal advice.

This reputation helped Delaware attract more than a dozen out-of-state banks such as Chase Manhattan and J. P. Morgan when the 1981 Financial Center Development Act offered tax incentives, lower operating costs, and eliminated the ceiling on interest rates.

Sporting an ostrich-skin jacket and duPont genes, Gerret Copeland studies the playbill at the Wilmington Grand Opera House. The 1871 opera house was restored in 1976 as Delaware's Center for the Performing Arts. It hosts OperaDelaware and the Delaware Symphony, as well as nationally touring performers.

Oblivious to their gilded surroundings, newlyweds Christopher and Carole Pitcher dance in the Gold Ballroom of the Hotel du Pont. Opened in 1913 as an extension of the new 12-story headquarters of E.I. du Pont de Nemours and Company, the 280-room hotel is renowned for its cuisine and an art collection that includes three generations of the Brandywine River Valley's most famous family, the Wyeths.

The annual Barefoot Ball of the Delaware Theater Company sizzles under a portrait of Marilyn Monroe, inspired by her performance in Some Like it Hot. Delaware's only professional theater company throws the ball — where most dance in shoes, actually — to raise money for its intern scholarships, summer acting camp, and other educational programs it offers around the state. Founded in 1979, the company opened a new theater overlooking the Christina River in 1988.

Backstage at the Playhouse, part of the Hotel du Pont, a young actress prepares to go on with a national touring company performance of *Gypsy*. Sarah Bernhardt, Bette Davis, and George C. Scott have walked the stage of the Playhouse, as did 10 horses and 20 foxhounds in its 1913 inaugural play, *The Whip*.

Not just for kids anymore, Halloween in Wilmington summons revelers to Loop Night. Flintstones cartoon characters point their car toward the next of several refreshment stops along the Loop, a downtown route reserved for pedestrians.

Frank Mearns and Beth Bradley forget auld acquaintance at a New Year's Eve charity ball given by the Dolphin Club, an affiliation of young New Castle County professionals who this night raised 3,600 dollars for the American Red Cross.

Breaking away in the Tour Du Pont,
a cyclist climbs Monkey Hill near
Wilmington's Brandywine Zoo. Teams
of some 130 competitors race through
towns across the mid-Atlantic in May
to complete eleven events.

Operated by Medalist Sports of
Virginia, the tour is underwritten by the
Du Pont Company, which awards
$300,000 in cash and prizes, and makes
over 40 of the products used by the
racers — from the Lycra in their
spandex shorts to the Kevlar reinforcing
their bike frames.

Rebounding from I-95, which razed sections of residential downtown Wilmington, the city found a perfect basketball court under the interstate girders at Third Street. About 60 percent black, the city's close-knit neighborhoods are also rich in Italian, Greek, Polish, Jewish, and Hispanic cultures. On a sunny sit-on-the-front-step kind of day, sisters Michelle and Shatira Robinson (above) throw smiles to passersby.

The week-long St. Anthony's Festival — attended by 300,000 people each June — closes with the Procession of the Saints, led by the Blessed Mother and Child. Along the parade route through west Wilmington, Ernest "Chew-Chew" Manucci sells holy cards to benefit the parish church, St. Anthony of Padua, the heart of the city's Italian community.

Protector of children, such as float riders Laura Kolodgie and Nicholas Desnars (above) St. Anthony is also believed to help find lost items. He doubtless hears many prayers from the festival's crowded midway, chocked with amusement rides, home-cooked food, and entertainment.

Sticky business wraps up a cotton candy vendor at the
Wilmington Flower Market, a three-day carnival of
food, crafts and rides that grew from a May flower
sale first held in 1921. Proceeds benefit charities for
Delaware children. The site is 104-acre Rockford Park,
designed by the creator of New York's Central Park,
Frederick Law Olmstead.

Tapping tanks of crude oil, Star
Enterprises in Delaware City can refine
140,000 barrels a day. Tankers dock at
the Delaware River port to deliver
crude, and leave with gas and heating
oil for clients throughout the Northeast.
Opened in 1957 by the Tidewater Oil
Company, the refinery has since been
operated by Getty, Texaco, and now Star
— created in a Texaco divestiture. Plans
by Shell to build another refinery were
blocked by the state's 1971 Coastal
Zone Act, which bars further heavy
industry from the shoreline and the
Chesapeake and Delaware Canal.

Dockworkers guide drums of lemon juice concentrate to a safe landing at the Port of Wilmington. One of the world's top orange juice ports, Wilmington is now the top banana port as well — handling over 50 million boxes in 1991, up from 11 million in 1985. Among the 4.7 million tons of imports and exports that annually pass through the port are 150,000 cars. Wilmington is the largest port of export for American-made cars. For Volkswagen, it is the major gateway to North America.

One of the nation's most advanced
automotive plants, Chrysler's Newark
Assembly Plant uses 238 robots and
an automatic framing and welding
system. Still, it couldn't produce 1,004
cars a day without 3,800 skilled
employees such as George Smith, left,
and Ron Thompson, affixing trim to
a Le Baron convertible. More than six
million cars have rolled out of the plant
since it opened in 1957.

This output, added to that of the
General Motors plant in nearby
Newport, makes automobiles one of
Delaware's largest industries.

Piled in seven-ton stacks, silver bars in the vault of Wilmington Trust represent only a fraction of the weighty responsibility borne by one of the world's largest custodians of precious metals. The bank has separate rooms for silver, gold, platinum, and palladium deposited here by brokerage houses, commodities dealers, and individual investors.

Precious metals delivered here for storage are not subject to sales tax, no matter where in the U.S. they were purchased.

Preparing to inoculate a young rice plant with fungus spores at the Du Pont Company's Experimental Station, molecular geneticist Barbara Valent investigates ways to control rice blast, chief destroyer of the staple food for half the world. As members of the station's Life Science's Molecular Plant Pathology Group, Dr. Valent and colleagues are working to develop environmentally safe fungicides and experimenting with varieties of rice. "Controlling this disease in an environmentally safe manner," she says, "is very important to the world."

One of the first research laboratories in the country, the 147-acre Experimental Station opened in 1903 and today employs 1,700 scientists. It's achievements are household words: nylon, Teflon, Lucite, Kevlar.

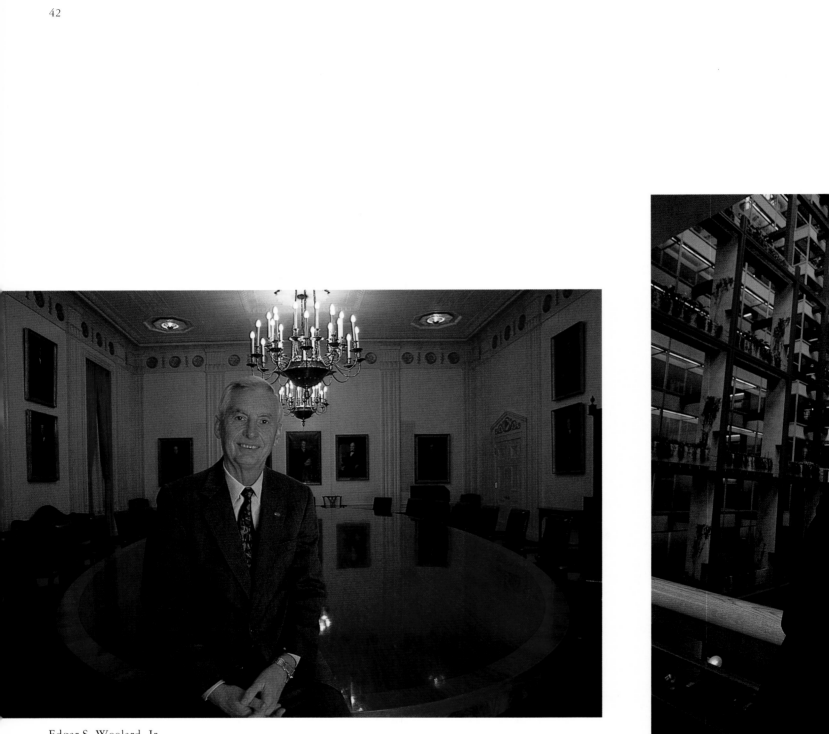

Edgar S. Woolard, Jr.,
Du Pont Company

Thomas L. Gossage,
Hercules Incorporated

The CEO of Du Pont — America's largest chemical company, the CEO of Hercules — the thirteenth largest, and the CEO of ICI Americas, the U.S. subsidiary of the fourth largest chemical company in the world, all make their offices in Wilmington. Why? Gunpowder. Du Pont controlled two-thirds of the U.S. gunpowder market when a federal court ordered it to divest in 1912; it spun off the Hercules Powder Company and the Atlas Powder Company.

Bernard H. Lochtenberg,
ICI Americas, Inc.

Du Pont had established its first chemical department a year earlier. Its pioneer explorations in the field were later followed by Hercules, maker of solid rocket propellants, polypropylene fiber, and advanced composite materials. In 1971, London-based Imperial Chemicals Industries bought Atlas, which became ICI Americas Inc., which manufactures products ranging from life-saving heart drugs to fully biodegradable plastics. All three corporations manufacture most of their products outside of the state.

Minutes north of Wilmington's city limits the land takes a pastoral turn, sprouting Holsteins, corn, and homes such as Granogue, a 515-acre du Pont family estate built in 1923 and still farmed. It's name may be French, Irish, or a local American Indian word.

Other du Pont estates in Chateau Country reflect place names where the family and relations lived in France and Switzerland before Pierre Samuel du Pont de Nemours brought them to the U.S. in 1800. Today his far-flung U.S. progeny — their collective worth perhaps 8.5 billion dollars — number more than 2,500 and live largely outside Delaware. None has controlling stock interest in their namesake company.

Heir apparent to an American art dynasty, Jamie Wyeth cradles his pet goose Lucy on his farm that straddles the Delaware-Pennsylvania border. His oil portrait of her hangs in Chicago's Tarra Museum of American Art. Jamie's grandfather, famed illustrator N. C. Wyeth, studied in Wilmington as a young man with Howard Pyle, a founder of the Brandywine School of Art. Jamie's father, Andrew Wyeth, has been described as "the quintessential painter."

Drawn to the spirit of animals, Wilmington sculptor Andrè Harvey completes a clay model of a frog to be cast in bronze. "What I try to do," he says, "is to put heart and soul into the metal."

Bounding over a 3.8-mile steeplechase,
thoroughbreds run for the sport of it
at the Winterthur Point-to-Point
Races. The gardens of the 963-acre
estate are in peak bloom for the annual
May fund-raiser for Winterthur, once
the private home of Henry Francis
du Pont — the fifth generation to own
it — and since 1951 a museum holding
his unsurpassed collection of American
decorative arts.

Active in collecting furnishings and
art for the museum until his death
in 1969, du Pont sat on the board of
the Du Pont Company. But for his
50th college reunion record he wrote:
"I have engaged principally in activities
which may not be of much interest to
my classmates: collecting American
antiques and farming at my place in
Delaware."

Fishy dishes landed a yellow ribbon in the Tailgate Picnic Competition at the Winterthur Point-to-Point for Joe Sailer, Susan Sanders, Amy Mulligan, Claude Auerback, and Liz Sanders.

To celebrate Yuletide, the museum concocted lady finger sponge cake, trifle, meringues, sweet meats, and a dried-fruit pyramid. The 19th-century dessert table is displayed at the base of the Montmorenci Staircase, brought to Winterthur from an 1822 North Carolina estate.

"I beg you not to let out any contract for supplying your powder magazines before you have compared what we are making with others."

Uncertain of his son's ambitions to make gunpowder, Pierre Samuel du Pont wrote these words to his friend, newly elected president Thomas Jefferson. When Hagley Mills opened in 1803, Jefferson directed the Secretary of War to place an order. Eleuthère-Irénée du Pont's French gunpowder formula was, in fact, superior. By the Civil War, E.I. du Pont de Nemours and Company was the nation's largest gunpowder producer.

Today explosives spark a mere fraction of Du Pont's profits, and Hagley, closed in 1921, is a museum of early American industry. The boxcar beside the graining mill (right) ran on wooden rails — a precaution against sparks that might trigger explosions. But, though infrequent, tragedies did occur. In March 1818 "forty souls were hurled into an unknown eternity," wrote Elizabeth Montgomery, a resident of nearby Wilmington, where the noise "burst upon the ear like the report of a cannon."

E. I. du Pont set up an annuity for each widow. His wife and brother-in-law were also injured by the blast, but the family continued to live in their home on the site, Eleutherian Mills, now preserved — explosion cracks and all — as part of the museum.

The Civil War flares anew during a
reenactment weekend at Hagley. No
Civil War battles bloodied the Union
state, but Fort Delaware gained infamy
as a prison camp. The Battle of
Gettysburg swelled its population to
perhaps 12,500 Confederate captives; as
many as 2,400 died.

Also imprisoned were Delawareans
suspected of sympathizing with the
South, as many did. The state never
relied heavily on African slave labor,
yet it was one of the last to free slaves
after the war.

North of Wilmington, Brandywine
Creek State Park (following pages) fires
volleys of autumn color. A stone wall
bordering the 795-acre refuge was
built by Italian stone masons when the
property was a du Pont dairy farm.

In an age of malls, Delaware still finds room for the general store. "You can find it at Wassam's" is the motto of this emporium in the colonial town of New Castle. Six thousand people are said to have attended the 1880 dedication of the building, then a hardware and feed store with a Masonic opera house upstairs.

It's been 150 years since anyone laid down fare at the ticket office of the New Castle and Frenchtown Railroad (above). Opened in 1831, the 16.5-mile-long track between Delaware Bay and Frenchtown — on the Chesapeake Bay's Elk River — saw cars pulled by horses for a year until a steam engine could be shipped from England. Railroads linking Wilmington with Philadelphia and Baltimore in 1838 brought about New Castle's decline as a port.

Sloops moor off New Castle's Battery
Park, where William Penn landed
in the New World in 1682 to claim his
grant to Delaware. He had requested that
the Duke of York add this land to
his Pennsylvania grant to guarantee sea
access via Delaware Bay.

The bay had been named for Lord
De La Warr, governor of Virginia in the
early 1600s. The name was only
gradually used for the colony, officially
called the Counties of New Castle,
Kent, and Sussex on the Delaware —
or, more commonly, the Lower
Counties of Pennsylvania.

Soon after Penn's arrival the Calverts
of Maryland protested that Delaware
fell under their grant. Along with the
written arguments for his case, Penn
shrewdly sent King Charles II "Beavers
& Otters for Hatts and Muffs."

By the time the Penn family won
the case — not long before the
Revolutionary War — Delaware had
had its own legislature for decades.
In accordance with the terms of Penn's
initial grant, the boundary between
Pennsylvania and Delaware is an arc
of a circle with a 12-mile radius drawn
from New Castle. The unique circular
border was measured from the spire
of the New Castle Court House,
Delaware's first capitol and a
centerpiece of the town's colonial
charms.

The granite pentagon of Fort Delaware last saw action during World War II, when the Army inducted part of the state's National Guard as the Separate Coast Artillery Battalion. But no battle shots were ever fired here. The fortress is now a war museum, having left the nation's security to the likes of the Estocin (above), a guided-missile frigate passing Ship John Lighthouse on its way from Philadelphia Naval Base. The state itself hasn't seen a military attack since the War of 1812, when a British warship bombarded the southern Delaware Bay harbor of Lewes, killing a chicken and injuring a pig.

Streaking toward home base at the
New Castle County Airport, a Delaware
Air National Guard pilot maneuvers a
Lockheed C-130 Hercules cargo plane.
Members of the 166th Tactical Airlift
Group may be required to mobilize
on short notice to take their place with
active Air Force units. Its pilots were
among the first to bring supplies
to Kuwait at the end of Desert Storm.

Following pages: Practicing for
Middletown's Police Athletic League
games, Richard Meadows and Theo
Anderson spar on a homemade
basketball court while aspiring barber
Nelson Meadows practices his future
trade. In this small state of
predominately small towns, "An
individual," says one resident, "can
leave his stamp on something."

Firewood and a coal bucket recall hot times at a former International Order of Oddfellows Lodge, built in 1914 in Bear. Little more than a crossroads, Bear used the lodge as a schoolhouse after its own burned down

in 1934. Today it's the residence of Jim Williams and family. Renovating the structure he found a dozen Indian costumes — probably the regalia of another fraternal order called the Redmen.

The image of simplicity, the Friends
Center Meeting House in Centerville
was built in 1796 and still holds
Sunday services. Quakers were active in
laying out Wilmington in the 1730s,
and dominated New Castle County's
early mill industries along the
Brandywine.

Delaware is considered the "cradle of
Methodism" in America. A 1784
meeting in Kent Country between a
British representative of John Wesley
and Francis Asbury led to a conference
in Baltimore, where the Methodist
Episcopal Church was founded.
Opposed to slavery, Methodist circuit-
rider ministers reached out to blacks as
well as whites. A former Kent Country
slave, Richard Allen, launched the
African Methodist Episcopal Church,
one of the largest black denominations
today.

Because of the influence of Quakers
and Methodists, many landowners
became Abolitionists, and Wilmington
became an important "station" on the
Underground Railroad. By the time of
the Civil War, only a small percentage
of Delaware's black population were
slaves.

72

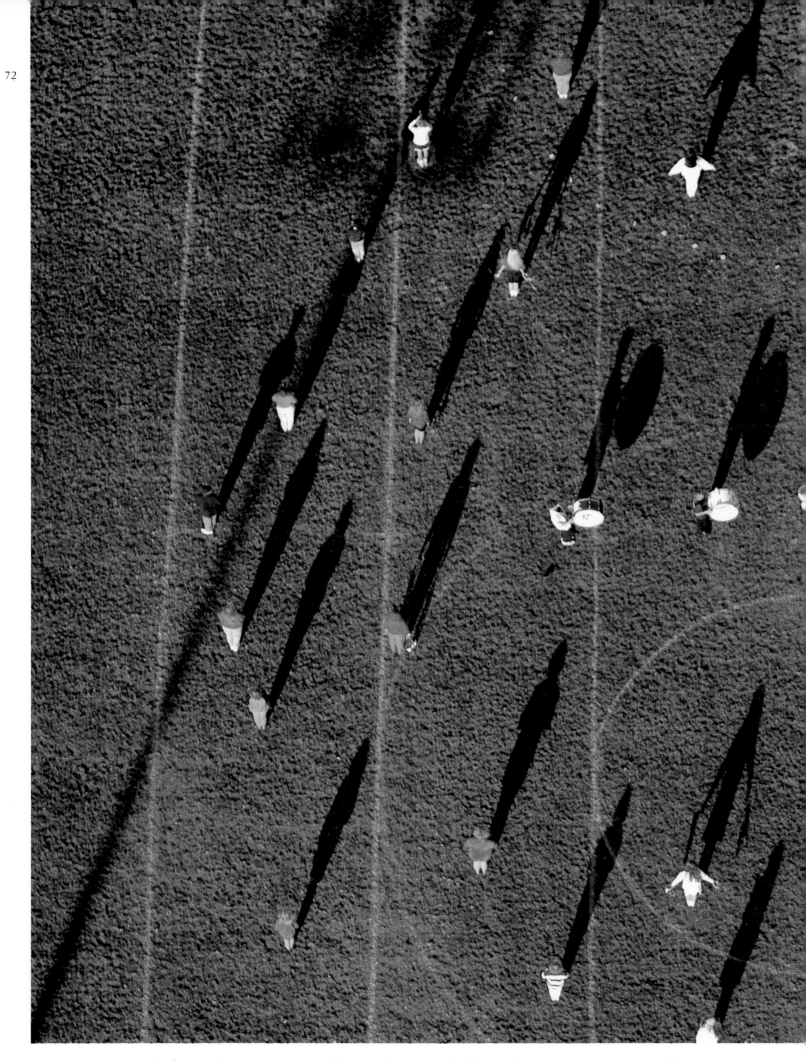

Halftime shadows march with the Glasgow High School Red Dragon Band, nationally recognized for excellence. Following pages: Precision practice makes perfect for the University of Delaware's Fightin' Blue

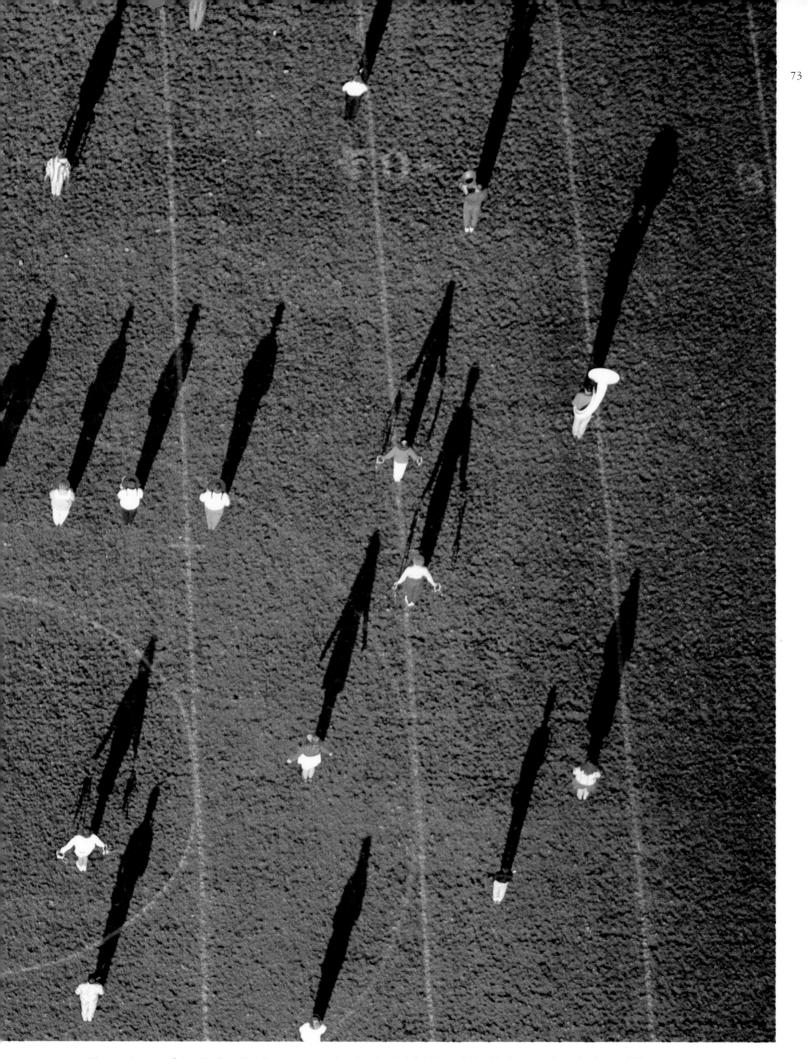

Hens, winners of the Yankee Conference championship in 1986, '88, and '91. Delaware's Revolutionary War troops earned the name "Blue Hen's chickens" for fighting as fiercely as gamecocks.

Instilling a sense of history, the Convocation welcomes more than 3,600 freshmen to the University of Delaware in Newark. Largest of the state's seven universities and colleges, it enrolls nearly 21,000 under-graduates, graduate students, and continuing education students here and on campuses elsewhere in the state, such as the College of Marine Studies in Lewes.

Autumn boughs shade the fluted columns of Memorial Hall, the original 1834 building of New Ark College, from which the University was born in 1921.

The chemistry is right for good times when the University of Delaware heats up for Homecoming Weekend. The school is especially noted for its departments of chemistry, engineering, and art, but Homecoming brings out a special creativity too. Come Monday, it's back to the drawing board for Dr. Dana Chatellier's science lecture.

If this is Ogletown it must be
Oktoberfest — a three-day microcosm
of Munich's three-week festival, hosted
by the 800 members of the Delaware
Saengerbund. More than 19,000 visitors
pass through the festival's circus tent
for beer, bratwurst, and entertainment
such as the whirling Enzian
Volkstanzgruppe, the Saengerbund's
folk dancing group, named after a tiny
blue Alpine flower. Formed in 1853,
the Saengerbund, or singing club, is the
hub of Delaware's German-American
community.

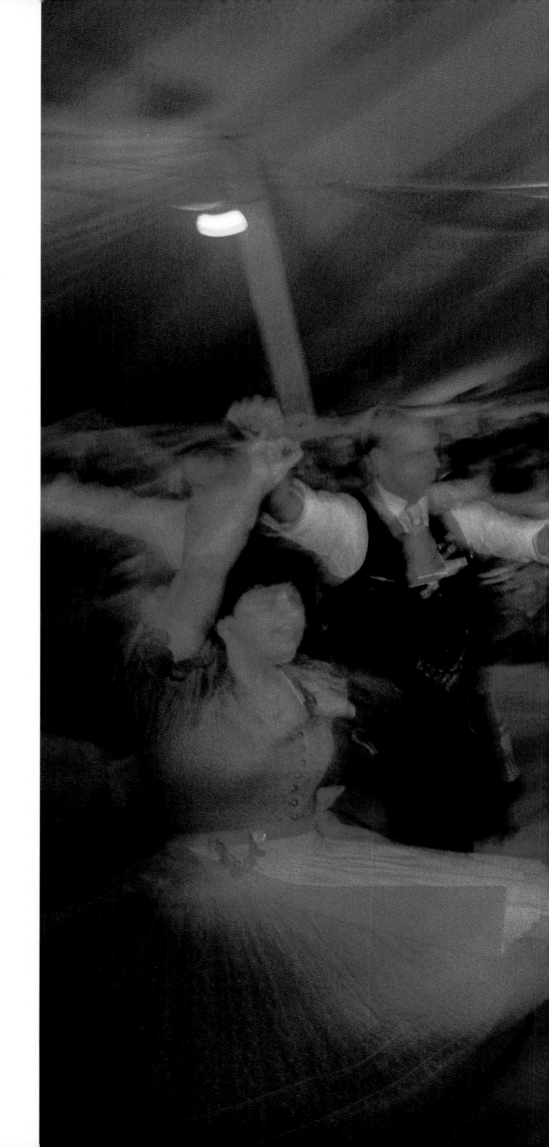

Sixty-five yards of ribbon and a pickup-truck of greens go into the wreath Sal DePaulo hangs each Christmas on his 1844 barn near Centerville. Following pages: It takes Rick Faucher and family nearly three months to

cover their house in Red Lion with 697,812 Christmas lights — and $1,600 a month to pay the electric bill.

"We do it for the love of children," says Faucher, who has been named the official state Santa.

Well dressed in all seasons, historic Odessa was called Cantwell's Bridge before it took the name of the famous Black Sea grain port in the mid 19th century. In the early 1800s this Delaware Bay town on Appoquinimink Creek grew prosperous shipping wheat, corn, and tobacco. But the 1855 opening of the Delaware Railroad — which ship owners had refused to allow to run through Odessa — shifted the focus of commerce. Not even the symbolic name change could lure business back.

A tannery established here in 1765 by William Corbit also went bust. His profits had built the beautiful Corbit-Sharp House, preserved today, along with the 1769 Wilson-Warner House and its stone barn (above), as part of Winterthur Museum.

The dam of the Edgar Hoopes Reservoir (preceding pages) holds back two billion gallons of water diverted from the Brandywine River as an emergency water supply for Wilmington. Completed in 1932, the 192-acre

reservoir (above) was excavated from a natural valley northwest of the city, and named in memory of a former
chief engineer of the Wilmington Water Department.

Using every square foot of valuable
agricultural land available, a farmer near
Middletown turns his home and
outbuildings into an island in the field.
Most of New Castle County below the
Chesapeake and Delaware Canal remains
farmland.

KENT

Fourth of July lights up Legislative
Hall in Dover. The state's General
Assembly first met in Dover in 1777
when British troops threatened New
Castle; the capital was officially
transferred in 1781. So it was in Dover
that Delaware became the First State,
by being first to ratify the U.S.
Constitution on December 7, 1787.

"What the Delaware convention did
from its convening on December 3
until its action and adjournment on
December 7 is not wholly known,"
wrote Delaware historian John Munroe.
"No hint of a debate on the merits of
the Constitution has survived." But
former governor Pierre S. "Pete"
du Pont IV (1977-1985) shared this
entertaining theory with visitors: "Look
at the bar bill at Mrs. Battel's tavern
and you'll understand exactly what was
going on. The crops were in, their wives
were saying it was time to do winter
chores, and they said, 'I'm going to
Dover for a few days and talk about
freedom and independence.' They ate
and drank and at the end said, 'Aye.'
And we had the beginning of a nation."

The front porch peacefulness of Dover lets Gary Patterson and daughter Seton pass a weekend reading (preceding pages), and is surprisingly undisturbed by neighboring Dover Air Force Base, home to the world's largest aircraft, the C-5B. A third of the 120-plane U.S. fleet is stationed here, but flight paths are chosen carefully. Coinciding with its 50th anniversary, the base was selected as best in the Air Force in 1991. Designed to carry outsize equipment, Dover's C-5B's saw action in Desert Storm and later airlifted food and supplies to refugee Kurds. To a changing Russia the fleet brought aid during Operation Provide Comfort and Operation Provide Hope.

Air Force pilots coming into Dover during Desert Storm saluted with barrel rolls and wing tilts when they passed over the Harrington barn painted by Clarence Barlow (following pages).

Raising a checkered flag signals a fan's personal victory: surviving the NASCAR Budweiser 500. The end-of-May race draws 77,000 people to Dover Downs International Speedway; many camp out for the full weekend of activities.

The high-banked track challenges stock cars masters such as (preceding pages) Folger Ford driver Mark Marvin, Kodak Film Chevy driver Ernie Irvan, and 1991 NASCAR champ Dale Earnhardt — supercharged even when his fans aren't (left). Dover Downs revs up again in late September for the PEAK Antifreeze 500.

Fifty years old and still running strong, an International H tractor driven by Harold Powell casts a shadow
on the old dairy barn of Tappahanna Marsh Plantation near Hartly (preceding pages). Honored as a Delaware
Century Farm, it has been in his family since 1874.

Agricultural traditions passed down at the Delaware State Fair include the Pretty Animal Contest and
showing prize animals. Phillip Busker's Holstein (left) took third and fifth place in its class. More than
200,000 people stroll the Harrington fairgrounds and midway each July. One untraditional aspect: The fair is
not funded by the state but is a nonprofit organization, incorporated as the Kent and Sussex Fair in 1919.

The State Fair pie eating contest puts a graham-cracker smile on a banana-cream face. In Delaware's agricultural pie, poultry accounts for nearly 69 percent, corn and soybeans grown for chicken feed 12 percent, and livestock nearly 7 percent. Vegetables — led by potatoes, fruits — led by melons, and dairy products account for the rest.

Sleeping with the cows during the fair keeps them calm, and shows you've done your job to prepare them for judging. Though only one half of one percent of the state's population are farmers, agriculture remains Delaware's top industry. Slightly less than half the land is devoted to agriculture, the largest percentage on the East Coast.

A creamy fog floats over Delaware's largest dairy farm, the 2,000-acre Thomas Farm outside Marydel. With fields of wheat, soybeans, and hay it nourishes its own 420 Holsteins and sells feed to others. Ninety percent of

the state's tilled acreage grows soybeans and corn. Following pages: Feed corn brings the best price when dry.
When the stalks are golden, a farmer near Smyrna begins his harvest.

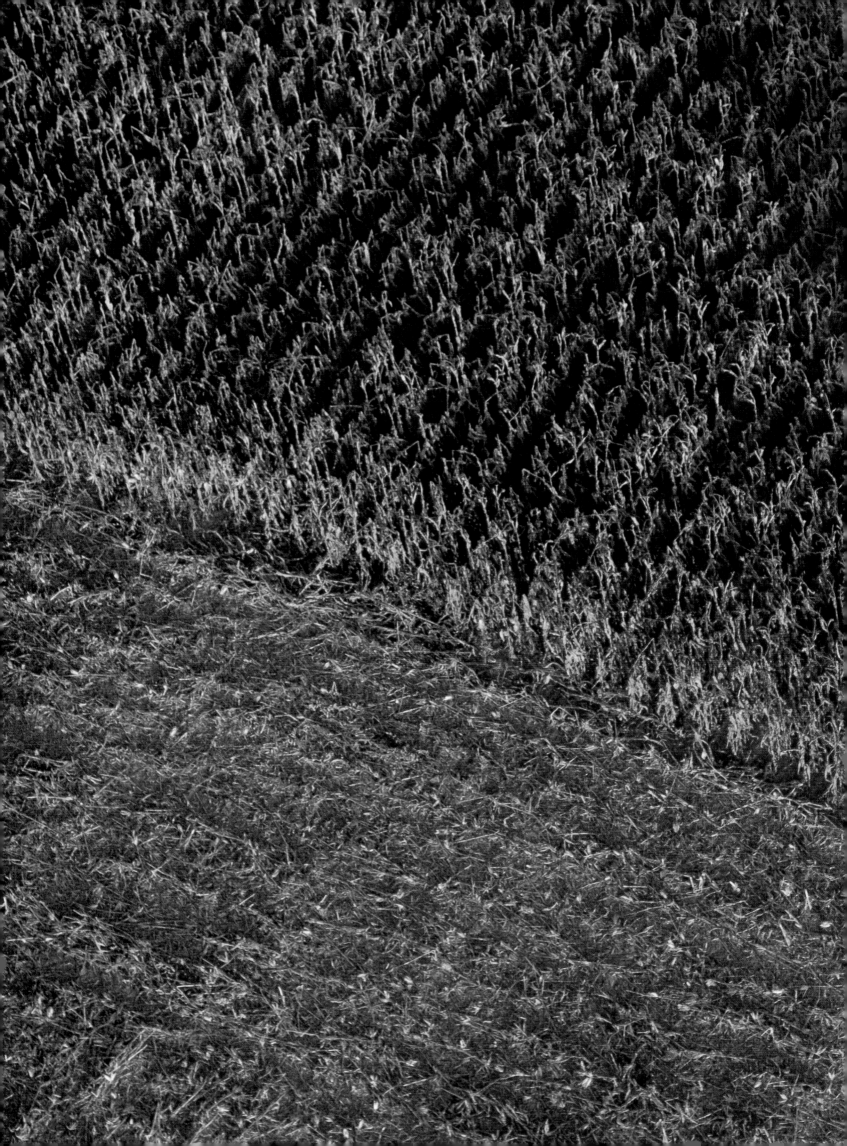

No agricultural dinosaur, the Zimmatic pivot irrigation system waters fields of vegetables, melons, and corn — showering arcs of water more than 50 feet. As harvest time approaches, grain growers shut down their irrigation systems and pray for sunny skies and dry nights so their crops can be picked with little moisture content. Their harvest, trucked to nearby grain elevators, is sold at market prices or stored in massive silos. Most of Delaware's grain feeds the local poultry industry.

Not impulse shoppers, members of Kent Country's Old Order Amish community consider equipment offered at a sale benefiting their local Amish school, Rose Valley. About 130 Old Order Amish live west of Dover, dwindling in number as farmland here becomes more valuable as real estate. Young couples seeking a traditional life are moving to communities in Michigan, Wisconsin, and Missouri.

Most Amish men are farmers, carpenters, or blacksmiths. Among the many skills of Amish women is preserving their farm's produce. Asked about her pantry inventory a mother of four replied: "203 quarts of applesauce, 75 quarts of peaches, 50 pints of peas, 40 pints of butter beans, 40 cans of tomatoes, 35 pints of sweet corn, and 40 quarts of string beans."

For casual conservation, Amish elders speak low German, the tongue Delaware's Amish use at home. High German is used in church services, English is taught in school.

When an out-of-gear tractor rolled out of place at the Rose Valley School sale, boy-power pushed it back. The Amish make allowances for gas-powered washing machines, but when it comes to field work, "We don't use modern conveniences; we stay with our old tradition and do everything with horse power," says Henry Byler, an Amish farmer near Cheswold.

The horse knows the way to carry the sleigh and the family Christmas tree on a farm near Cheswold. Many farmers grow Christmas trees to supplement their income from more traditional crops of corn and soy beans.

Embracing more than 15,000 acres along Delaware Bay, Bombay Hook National Wildlife Refuge cloisters deer and red fox in its timbered highlands (preceding pages) and wetlands.

Great egrets (right and following pages)
wade in Bombay Hook's tidal
marshlands, along with a annual
migration of 200,000 ducks and geese.
A haven for bird watchers, Delaware's
premier wildlife preserve is a vital
migratory stop on the Atlantic Flyway.

Canada geese rise with the sun over George's Island in Bombay Hook. Once Delaware's most prominent winter residents, Canada geese are now vastly outnumbered by snow geese. Flying from Arctic Circle islands, 150,000 snow geese settled across the state in winter 1991. A black duck stands out against some of the 40,000 who congregated in Bombay Hook (following pages). The huge flocks cause problems for the refuge with their eating habits: Pulling up vegetation by the roots creates mud flats and deprives Canada geese and ducks that merely graze. Extending the snow geese hunting season has helped the situation. Farmers have little problem with flocks that fly inland to pluck corn fields (pages 136-137) — the crop is already harvested.

A dawn rendezvous with blue crabs draws waterman Jack Grove down the Leipsic River toward Delaware Bay (preceding pages). Like many commercial crabbers — legally limited to 200 pots — he also nets fish and sets traps for eels, a more reliable profit.

The abandoned Catherine M. Lee (left) symbolizes the health of the bay's oyster industry, devastated in the 1950s by the parasite MSX. The 1992 oyster harvest was the first taken from the bay since 1985. A state research vessel, Ringold Brothers (above), patrols from Woodland Beach to Cape Henlopen to monitor the conditions of seeded oyster beds and fish populations.

More than 3,000 merchant ships and tankers a year travel along the shipping channel, dredged to counter heavy shoaling.

Leaving Bowers Beach and the mouth of the Murderkill River, a charter fishing boat wakes a sleepy Delaware Bay. Bowers Beach is the northernmost port of the state's multimillion dollar sportfishing industry. It also harbors commercial fishermen, though few do as their fathers did and trap muskrats as well. "We lived on fish and muskrats," remembers waterman Jack Donovan. "Mom could fix muskrat six nights a week and it'd never be the same. The gravy is out of this world."

SUSSEX

Summer transforms Rehoboth Beach into the hot
spot of Delaware's Atlantic coast resorts, and rockets
the town's year-round population of less than 5,000
to as many as 100,000. Methodists, envisioning a
"resort with religious influences," built Rehoboth's
first boardwalk in 1873. Violent winter storms in
1962 and 1992 destroyed sections of today's
promenade, slightly longer than a mile.

All of the state's 25-mile-long oceanfront lies in
Sussex County. Still predominantly rural, the county's
isolation on the Delmarva Peninsula was broken in
1952 when the Chesapeake Bay Bridge opened up a
tourist avenue of escape from Washington, D.C., and
Baltimore. Half the annual visitors to the state
vacation in Rehoboth, Bethany Beach, Dewey Beach,
Lewes, and Fenwick Island — and leave behind 250
million dollars.

The Lifeguard Olympics pit the 42
members of the Rehoboth Beach Patrol
against rescue teams from Ocean City,
Maryland, and other mid-Atlantic
resorts. The patrol's exceptional track
record allows Rehoboth to call itself one
of the Atlantic's safest beaches.

Following pages: The winners of the
Best Body on the Beach display their
champion forms.

Deep cover-ups and arresting romances: the summer reading is never boring on Rehoboth Beach's broad sands. Rehoboth Beach's terrain is unusual for a mid-Atlantic ocean site. The shore rises into solid, rocky ground that supports two natural freshwater lakes and groves of oak, loblolly pine, and holly — the state tree. An early ad slogan touted Rehoboth as the spot "where the pines meet the brine."

A sunrise benediction touches the lodestone of summer commerce: Boardwalk and Rehoboth Avenue. But
Rehoboth no longer hibernates in winter. A growing number of retirees support year-round shops and services,

which, in turn, attract more off-season visitors. The lure of affordable retirement property has made Sussex Country the fastest-growing region in the state.

An imposing but ephemeral crab palace placed first in the Rehoboth Beach Sand Castle Contest.

A contender for best surfing on the East Coast is the shore near Indian River Inlet (following pages), a broad cut between the ocean and the connecting Rehoboth and Indian River Bays.

Contestants in the East Coast Skimboarding Championships at Dewey Beach combine skills of surfing and gymnastics to execute triple flips and barrel rolls. Skimmers come from as far away as Australia, and range in age from four to forty. "It's like a family," says former Dewey Beach mayor Bruce Vavala, who helped start the contest in 1982. "The older ones help the kids."

Conducting the last rites of summer, a "Not Too Grim Reaper" leads an "Irreverent Crew of Mourners and Revelers" in a New Orleans-style jazz funeral procession on the boardwalk of Bethany Beach. The reaper, Moss Wagner, inaugurated the ceremony in 1987. His ice cream parlor is the hot night spot in this dry town. In accordance with jazz funeral tradition, the march begins on a mournful note and ends in joy, with a party at Moss's house.

Summer's end brings mixed feelings to residents of Delaware's shore. Says one native: "We live one life in summer and another life in the winter. You're always glad to see people come, and glad to see them go."

Surf casting from Dewey Beach at sunrise, Barry Cullen hopes to catch his evening meal (following pages). Fall and spring bring the best surf fishing for bluefish, sea trout, and flounder. But even during summer — when fishing is banned on crowded beaches — there's open casting from state parklands, which comprise more than half of Delaware's Atlantic shore.

Outriggers quill a threatening sky at Indian River Marina. Its 300 state-owned slips are rented by sportsfishermen, lobstermen, and boats that take scuba divers to offshore wreaks. April to November is top season for catches such as mako sharks, wahoo, black drum, marlin, tuna, and mahi-mahi (above). Thinking conservation, most fishermen release their catches.

A handful of professional clammers
drag their bull rakes along the bottom
of Rehoboth Bay — seven feet at its
deepest — harvesting by hand as the
law requires. After a 13-year moratorium,
neighboring Indian River Bay was
opened again to clamming in 1991.

Most of the traffic on these back bays
is for pleasure (preceding pages) —
an aquatic dance of power boats, jetskis,
windsurfers, and sailors. To the north,
an oil tanker and a Lewes-based fishing
boat exit Delaware Bay by Cape
Henlopen en route to the Atlantic.
(pages 168-169).

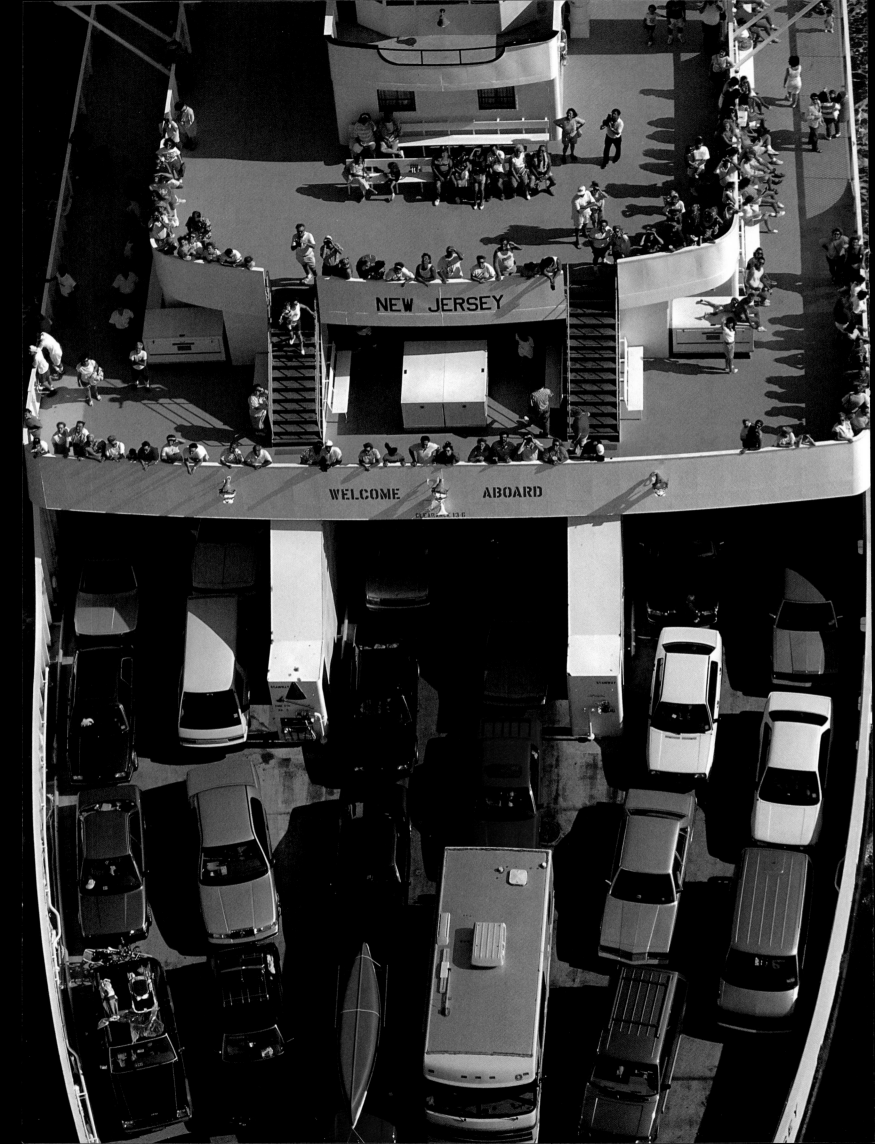

"There's a tremendous amount of talent on this boat," says a crew member of the Cape May-Lewes Ferry. Each has served in the Navy, Coast Guard, or Merchant Marine, and prides themselves in safely handling the five ferries, boarded by some 350,000 vehicles and a million passengers each year. The original ferry route across the mouth of Delaware Bay dates to 1793; modern operations began in 1964, after it was determined that traffic volume did not warrant a bridge. Travel time is 70 minutes, and crossings cease only if winds reach 65 miles-per-hour or the ferries experience a 12-degree roll.

Summer's dusk gathers a houseboat
party on the Lewes and Rehoboth
Canal. From this protected waterway off
Lewes's Delaware Bay harbor, charter
boats, head boats, and commercial
fishermen stream out to the bay and
Atlantic.

Delaware River Pilots, required by
law to escort merchant ships and
tankers up the estuary's shipping
channel, also make their headquarters
in Lewes, site of the state's first
settlement. In 1631, 28 Dutchman
posted a palisade and named the site
Zwaanendael — Valley of the Swans.
Conflict with local Indians made it a
short-lived venture, but by 1659 the
Dutch were back, putting down the
roots of today's port, population 2,200.

The Indians, who called themselves
Lenni Lenape, were part of a loose-knit
coastal culture of the Algonquin
language group. Attacked by northern
Iroquois tribes and pressured by
European settlement, most had moved
off the Delmarva Peninsula by the
1750s. Those who remained in Sussex
Country lived near their namesake
Nanticoke River, and today preserve
their history as the Nanticoke Indian
Association. Many East Coast tribes
join in their annual autumn powwow
in Oak Orchard.

Surrounded by his work, artist Howard
Schroeder brushes the sky of a new
painting in his Lewes studio. World
War II summoned Schroeder here to
Fort Miles, quickly built by the Army
on Cape Henlopen to protect the mouth
of the bay. A New York native,
Schroeder reenlisted as a Delawarean,
set up shop, raised six children, and
helped establish the Rehoboth Art
League. Wandering the dunes of Cape
Henlopen, now a state park, remains
his inspiration.

Other views that have inspired local
artists include the sunset silhouette of a
pine hummock on Herring Creek off
Rehoboth Bay (following pages).

Anna Cannon counts an afternoon with grandchildren as a blessing — no matter which Ninja Turtle young Antoine is pretending to be. And though first-grader Cirra "doesn't like getting her hair braided," says Anna, "she likes it when I'm done." Mother of eight and grandmother of 14, she sees small-town living in Laurel as another blessing: People don't think it's strange "to talk about the Lord."

In a quiet corner of southwest Sussex County, in the quiet town of Laurel, Nellie O'Neal makes a blooming splash. Named for the laurel bushes along Broad Creek, the town was launched in 1802 as a shipping port for produce. Today it's 3,500 residents work mainly in agriculture or in nearby Seaford at the world's largest nylon plant, opened by Du Pont in 1939.

Defying gravity, a 1923 barn endures
on the Briggs family farm east of
Georgetown, Sussex's county seat. "I've
had people want to purchase the
building just for the cedar board," says
Lewis Briggs, a Delaware State Police
detective and father of hoop shooters
Michael and Lewis, Jr. His brother
manages the farm, which delivers 3,000
ears of corn daily to summer produce
stands.

Kim White slings a sisterly arm over
Ronisha Frazier at the end of a long day
at the family's fruit stand in Ellendale.
Roadside vendors are a major crop in
Sussex County. For tourists driving to
the beach, the joy of picking out
peaches, fresh corn, and vine-ripened
tomatoes is as much a part of the trip as
the first jump in the surf.

There's a big advantage to small towns: Everyone gets to be the parade. The Bicycle Brigade in Bethany Beach and a free-for-all in Frankford raise the Fourth of July banner high.

Save for an accident of history, these southern Sussex towns would be celebrating in the state of Maryland. In the long border dispute between the Calverts and the Penns, it was agreed that the Penn's southern boundary was Cape Henlopen. But the map the Calverts submitted to the court in England incorrectly placed the cape some 25 miles south at Fenwick Island. The Penn's saw the error immediately, the Calverts too late. In 1751 surveyors drew the Transpeninsular Line to the center of the Delmarva Peninsula. From there, Charles Mason and Jeremiah Dixon drew Delaware's western border up to the arc, then continued their famous line west to separate Maryland and Pennsylvania.

Just as the peppers of summer (above) give way to the pumpkins of fall, fields of fruits and vegetables have given way to soybeans and corn: chicken feed for the state's top agricultural earner (following pages). The modern poultry industry — chickens raised as a year-round eating commodity — was hatched in Sussex County in 1923 by Cecile Steele of Ocean View. Broilers had long been shipped from here, but as a by-product of the fresh egg industry. Needing quick cash, Mrs. Steele quickly raised and sold a brood of 500 in the spring market. Her husband was so impressed with her business that he quit his Coast Guard lifesaving job at Bethany Beach to join it. Delaware now ranks eighth nationally in broilers, but no county produces more chickens than Sussex, more than 200 million a year.

"It's pretty good eatin', I'll tell ya," says Harry Banning, (above, at right) of the chicken he barbecues at the Kiwanis Club concession in Bridgeville. An eyewitness to the boom in beach-bound traffic, he's been basting with his secret sauce here since 1947. "You make friends, and it's nice to see them stop by again and again."

How many spicy chicken wings can you eat in half an hour? Cheered on, the winner of the second annual Wings To Go Starboard Chicken Eating Contest Beach put away 91, licked the special Suicide Hot Sauce off his fingers, and went out for a sundae. A Dover-based franchise, Wings to Go delivered 4,000 wings to Dewey's Starboard Restaurant for the July feast.

As much as 700 pounds of food fattens a hog during it's six-month lifetime, so feeding them keeps Joseph Donovan busy on Bill Walton's 21-acre Ellendale hog farm, the state's largest. "Those about to go to market get all the food they want," says Walton. Sussex Country raises most of Delaware's hogs, the second most important livestock after chickens.

"It's the biggest thing farmers have around here," says Marshall Hastings, left, sitting at the Laurel Auction Market with friend Lloyd Bradley. "One hundred percent owned by farmers," the 1,600-member cooperative sells more than 25 million dollars of produce each summer to brokers from Northeast markets.

It is often a long, hot wait during peak season in August for growers wanting to sell their crop at the Laurel Auction Market. Perhaps 100 farm trucks drive up to the block each day, carring anywhere from 50 to 500 melons. Watermelons dominate, followed by cantaloupes, honeydews, tomatoes, pumpkins, and other vegetables. Once purchased they must be transferred to the buyer's truck. After a day of tossing the equivalent of ten-pound footballs, it's not hard to understand why a teenager's breathless explanation of his summer job is simply, "I throw melons" (following pages).